W9-AJO-214

Dedicated to Nick, Tony, Riley, Hailey, and Lacey.

The Child's World

Published in the United States of America by The Child's World®
PO Box 326 • Chanhassen, MN 55317-0326
800-599-READ • www.childsworld.com

Acknowledgments
The Child's World®: Mary Berendes, Publishing Director; Katherine Stevenson, Editor
The Creative Spark, San Juan Capistrano, CA: Design and page production

Photos
© David M. Budd Photography

Copyright © 2007 The Child's World®
All rights reserved. No part of this book may be reproduced or utilized in any form
or by any means without permission from the publisher.

Library of Congress Cataloging-in-Publication Data
Pistoia, Sara.
  Money / by Sara Pistoia.
     p. cm. — (MathBooks)
  Includes index.
  ISBN 1-59296-689-6 (lib. bdg. : alk. paper)
  1. Counting—Juvenile literature. 2. Coins, American—Juvenile literature. I. Title.
  QA113.P566 2006
  513.2'11—dc22
                              2005037836

MathBooks

Money

By Sara Pistoia

The Child's World

How do we use money?

We use money to **buy** things. We give other people money, and they give us something in return. Using money is a form of **trading**.

Long ago, people did not use money. When they needed something, they traded other items or their time.

Today people use money instead. They sell items or they sell their time, and they get money in return. Then they use the money to buy things.

Did you ever trade things with your friends? Then you know what trading is all about!

Counting is important when you use money.

penny = one cent   nickel = five cents

Have you seen these coins?

dime = ten cents   quarter = twenty-five cents

Can you count these pennies?

Each penny is worth one cent.

You need to count by ones.

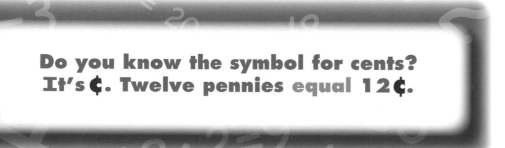

Do you know the symbol for cents?
It's ¢. Twelve pennies equal 12¢.

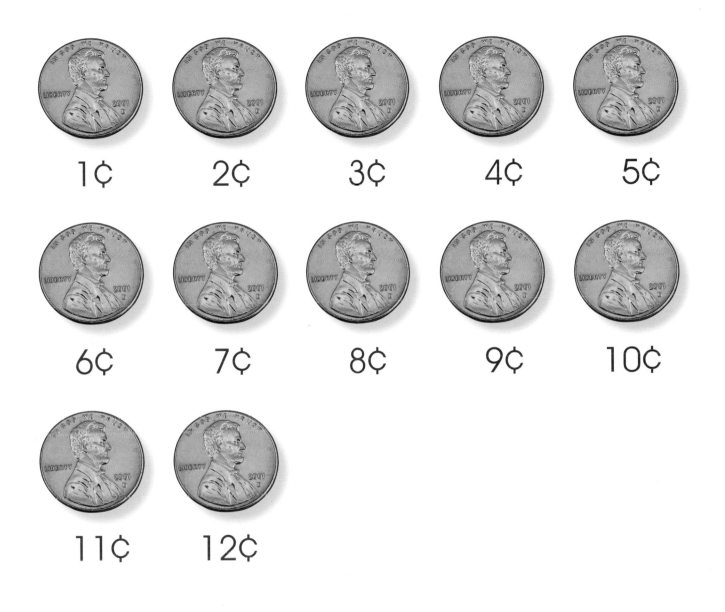

1¢ 2¢ 3¢ 4¢ 5¢

6¢ 7¢ 8¢ 9¢ 10¢

11¢ 12¢

Did you count to twelve? That means you have twelve cents.

Here are some nickels. Each nickel is worth five cents.

Can you count these nickels? You need to count by fives.

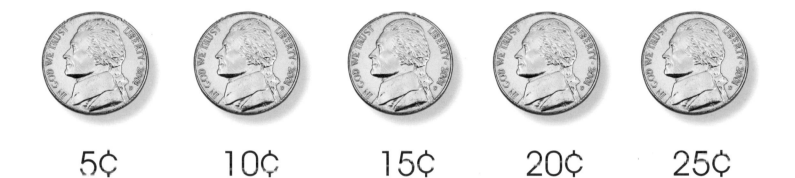

5¢   10¢   15¢   20¢   25¢

Did you count twenty-five cents?

A dime is worth ten cents. With dimes, you need to count by tens.

Try counting these dimes.

| 10¢ | 20¢ | 30¢ | 40¢ |

| 50¢ | 60¢ | 70¢ | 80¢ |

Wow! You have eighty cents!

This candy costs ten cents.

Do you have enough money to buy it?

When you have mixed coins to count, start with the highest value. A nickel is worth more than a penny, so it has a higher value.

How much are one nickel and five pennies worth? Are they the same as one dime?

Count to find out!

| 5¢ | 6¢ | 7¢ | 8¢ | 9¢ | 10¢ |

If you have one quarter, you have twenty-five cents. You could trade your quarter for other coins. What coins could you get?

Five nickels equal one quarter.

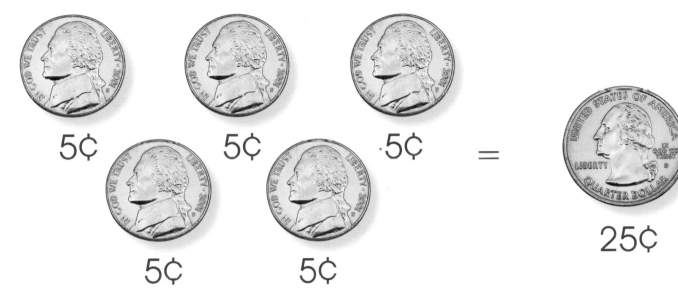

5¢   5¢   5¢   =   25¢

5¢   5¢

Two dimes and one nickel equal a quarter.

Count them and see!

10¢   10¢   +   5¢   =   25¢

Do you have enough money to buy this toy bear?

Start counting with the coin that is worth the most.

Finish with the coin that is worth the least.

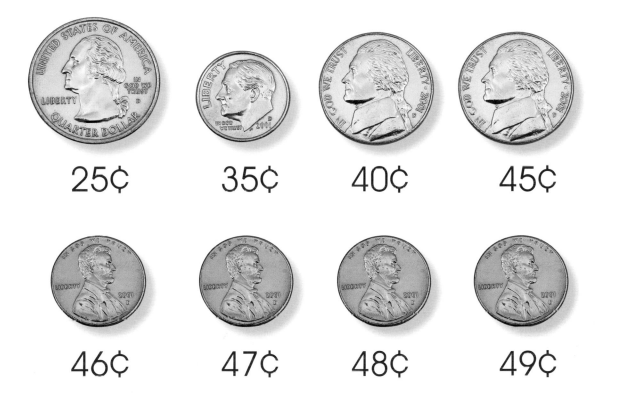

25¢   35¢   40¢   45¢

46¢   47¢   48¢   49¢

You didn't have enough money! What coin could you add so that you could buy the toy bear?

Do you **earn** money for helping at home? Count the coins you have earned by doing chores.

25¢   35¢   45¢   50¢

You might want to save your money so you don't spend it right away. Piggy banks are a great place to keep your money safe!

Money is part of our lives.

You can spend money and you can save money.

It's important to know how to count money!

Key Words

buy

cent

coins

dime

earn

equal

money

nickel

penny

quarter

trading

value

worth

Index

About the Author

Sara Pistoia is a retired elementary teacher living in Southern California with her husband and a variety of pets. After 40 years of teaching, she now contributes to education by supervising and training student teachers at California State University at Fullerton. In authoring this series, she draws on the experience of many years of teaching first and second graders.